Escape to Fairy Kingdom

For Aspen and Capri

Escape to Fairy Kingdom

Written & Illustrated
By Cazzy Zahursky

© copyright 2020

May was the only princess in her family's eyes.

Until mama brought home a tiny surprise.

Wherever May went, June tagged along,

Developing a bond, both special and strong.

But as the two sisters grew,

May got upset with June too.

Some days she felt frustrated.

Sometimes they had to be separated.

May whined when she had to share the last treat.

She was tired of having to behave so sweet.

May'd sigh when June wore her favorite shirt,

And returned it covered in paint or dirt.

June began taking May's toys without asking her first.

But it was June's imitating her, that made May feel the worst.

May asked, "Why does June have to copy everything I do?"

Her mama explained, "It's just because June loves you."

One evening May had enough

Of June touching her stuff.

So when May tore June's favorite bear,

May stormed off to her room, her nose in the air.

Knowing it was accidental,

May had shouted, "You need to be more gentle!"

Staring out the window, at the moon shining bright,

She felt so angry at June for ruining her night.

A shooting star went through the night sky.

May made a wish upon it as it shot by.

"I wish I could be all alone,

On my very own kingdom's throne."

Instantly, the night sky cleared,

And a fairy kingdom appeared.

Through May's window, in the distance,

A rainbow slowly came into existence.

A unicorn came rearing outside,
Offering her a magical ride.
It whispered, "I've come to take you far away.
This is your chance to escape with me, May!"

She rode through summer, fall, winter, and spring.

Until she heard the voice of a sweet fairy sing.

Then, a funny thing came about.

Upon May's back, wings began to sprout.

Arriving at the Fairy Kingdom, May couldn't believe her eyes.
It was filled with sweet treats of every flavor and size.
May thought about how much June would love this place,
Imagining a look of sheer joy on her face.

May was greeted by a fairy,

By the name of Vanillaberry.

"We have been waiting for you!

You're the perfect addition to our fairy crew!"

All they did was eat sweet treats and play.
And the fairies made May laugh every day.

Despite enjoying every treat in sight,

Something just...didn't feel quite right.

But sweet goodies were spread all over the place,

And May couldn't help but stuff her face.

Each and every day, they threw a party for May.

At some parties they sipped tea,

Nibbling on raspberry jam and Brie.

Sometimes they danced ballet,

Twirling all their troubles away.

Some parties went from dusk 'til dawn,
Out on the kingdom's Puppy Dog Lawn.

In May's honor they held a grand ball

In the castle's Great Bubble Gum Hall.

They offered her more riches than she'd ever seen.

And the fairies began treating her like a queen.

The fairies were glad

To share all that they had.

A fairy told May, "You must close your eyes.
We want to give you a special surprise."
They humbly bowed down,
Presenting her with an exquisite crown.
"Please stay with us forever and rule our fairy land.
All that you wish for will be our command.
We hope you will sit on our kingdom's throne.
We promise in exchange that you'll never be alone."

From atop a red and white toadstool,
She reached out to touch a sparkly jewel.
Her hand accidentally slipped down,
Breaking the magnificent crown.

The fairies were not the least bit mad,
But May still began to feel very bad.
She thought of June and her favorite toy bear.
That's when May realized she had been unfair.
With a feeling of regret,
Her eyes began to feel wet.

After all the sweet treats May rushed to devour,

Her stomach began to feel really sour.

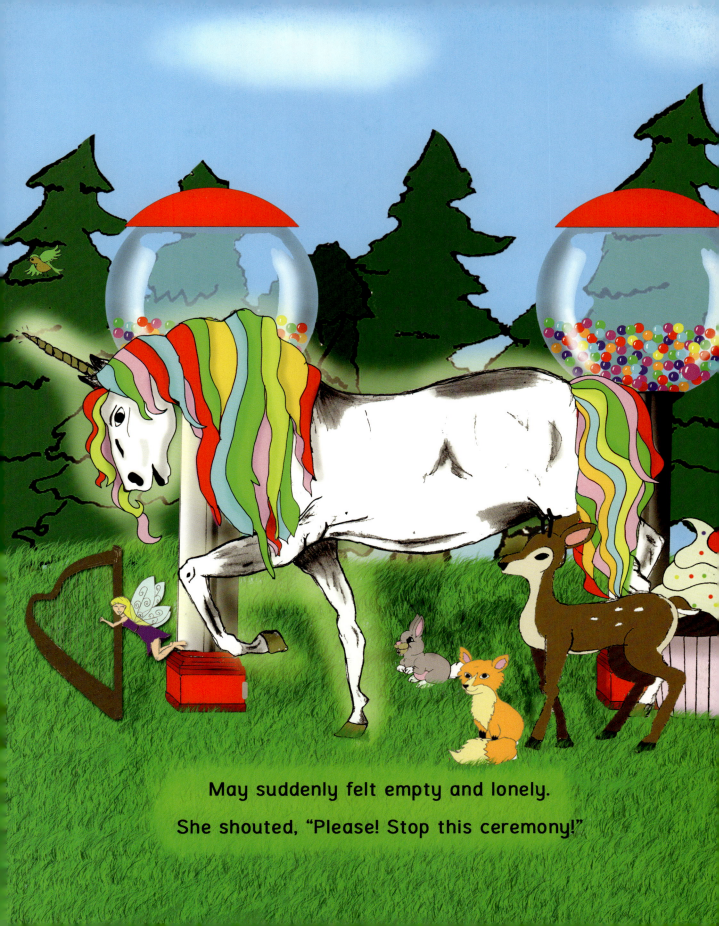

"Though becoming a queen

Was once my dream,

I was wrong all along.

I do not belong."

Tears fell down as she cried,

"Something has felt missing inside."

"What could possibly be missing?"

Asked a fairy above.

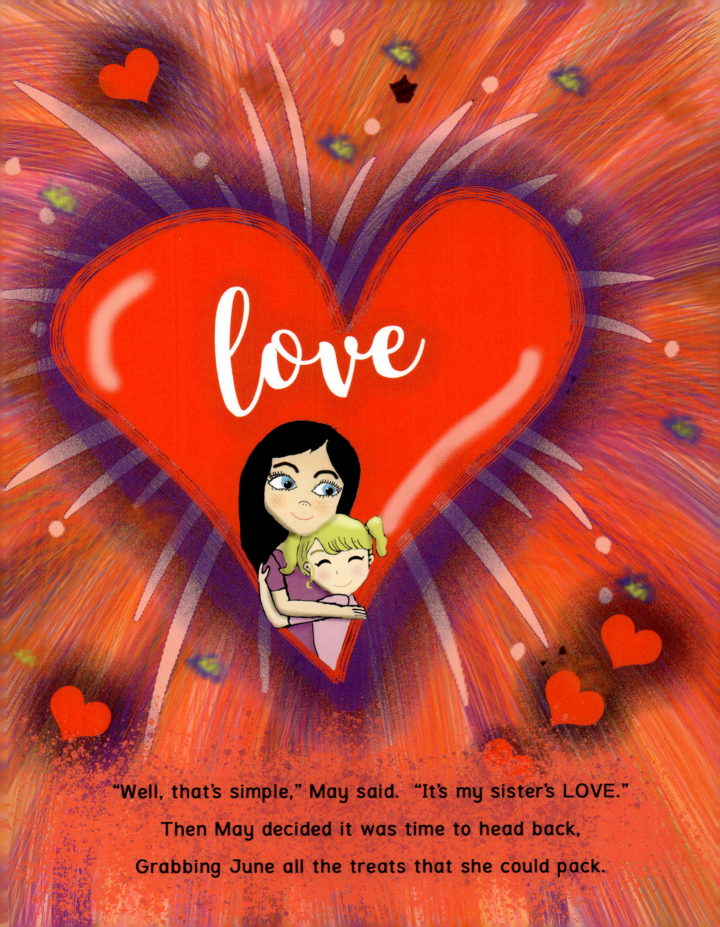

"Well, that's simple," May said. "It's my sister's LOVE."
Then May decided it was time to head back,
Grabbing June all the treats that she could pack.

May rode back through spring, winter, and fall,
Until she found the most important thing of all.

The warmth of June, her little sister.

The End

About the Author/Illustrator

Cazzy Zahursky is a wife and mother of two girls and two dogs. She enjoys spending time with her family, traveling, volunteering at her children's schools, and working out. She stays busy and inspired by her girls on a daily basis. She loves teaching them lessons through storytelling. Whether she's playing around with her girls or practicing yoga with her husband, she enjoys every memorable moment.

www.circletimebooks.com

Escape to Fairy Kingdom

Copyright ©2020 Cazzy Zahursky.
All Rights Reserved. No part of this publication may be reproduced, stored in a retrieval system or transmitted in any form by any means electronic, mechanical, or photocopying, recording or otherwise without permission of author.
All inquiries about this book can be sent to the author at info@circletimebooks.com
Published in Los Angeles, California by Circle Time Books, LLC

ISBN: 978-1-7342952-0-7

Library of Congress Control Number: 2020901498

Printed in USA